# BELONGS TO

○────────────────────────────○

# Name of the spell

--------------------------------

--------------------------------

**Time and place** --------------------------------

**Intention** --------------------------------

**Date** --------

SPELL

--------------------------------

--------------------------------

--------------------------------

--------------------------------

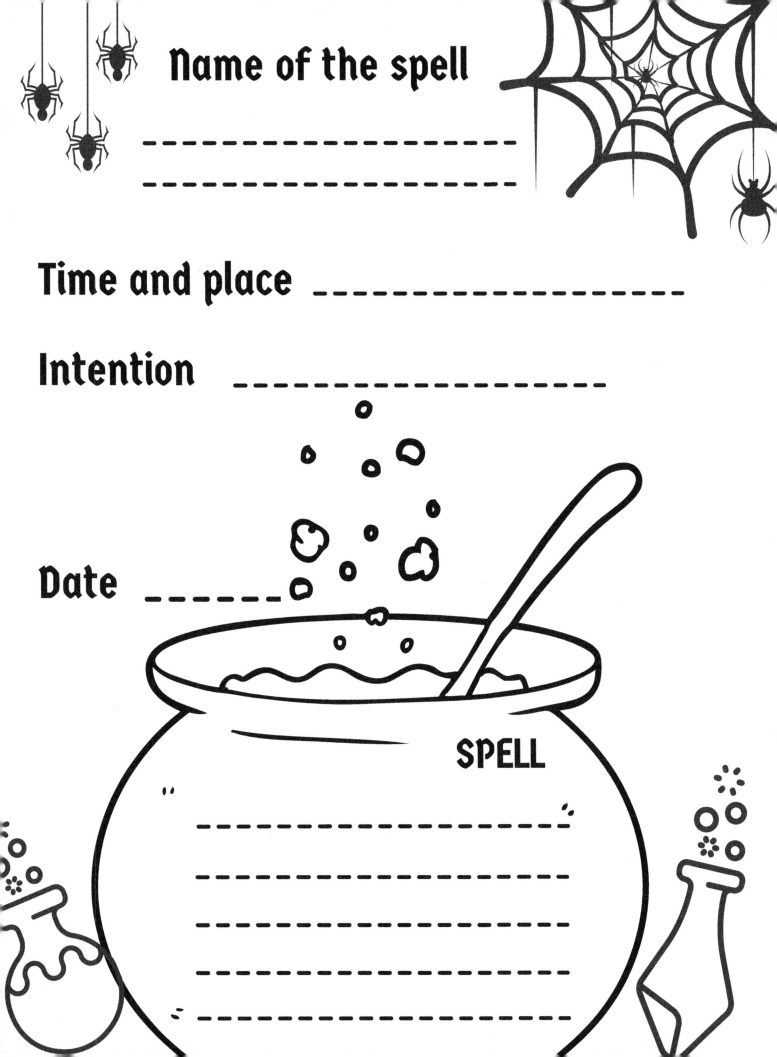

# Ritual

# Recipe

# Name of the spell

------------------------------

## Time and place

------------------------------

## Intention

------------------------------

### SPELL

------------------------------

------------------------------

------------------------------

------------------------------

------------------------------

------------------------------

## Date

# Ritual

# Recipe

# Name of the spell

--------------------------------

--------------------------------

**Time and place** --------------------------

**Intention** ----------------------------

**Date** -----------

SPELL

------------------------------

------------------------------

------------------------------

------------------------------

# Ritual

# Recipe

# Name of the spell

----------------------------------------

## Time and place

----------------------------------------

## Intention

----------------------------------------

### SPELL

----------------------------------------

----------------------------------------

----------------------------------------

----------------------------------------

----------------------------------------

----------------------------------------

## Date

# Ritual

## Recipe

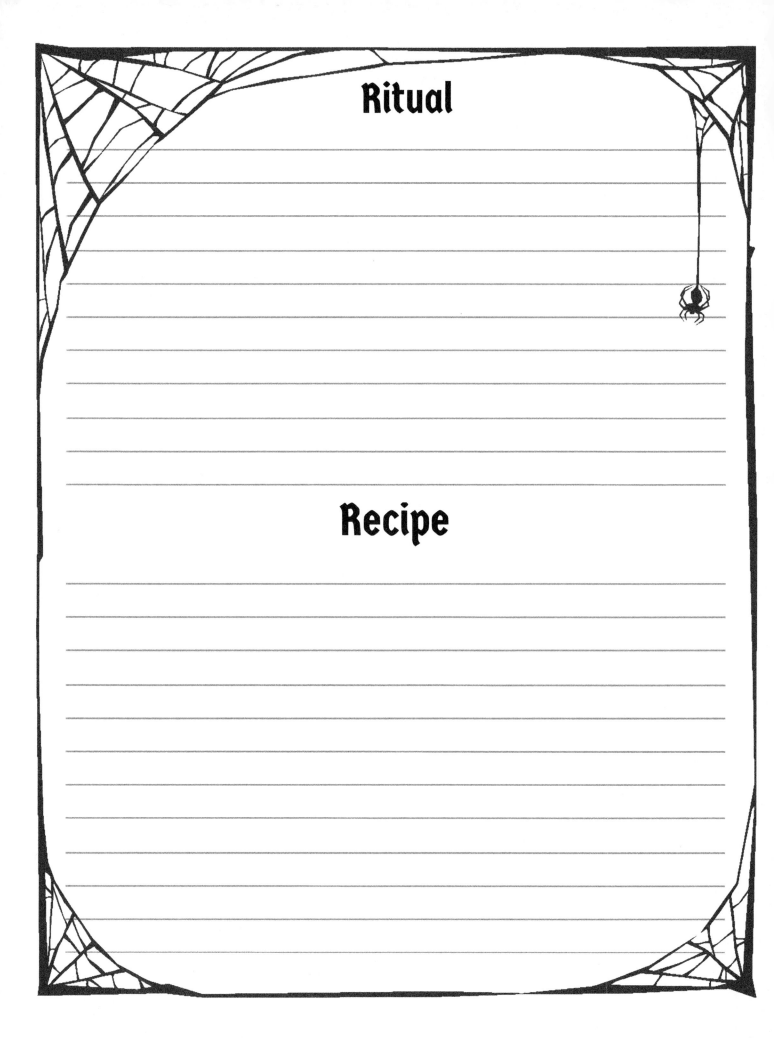

# Name of the spell

------------------------------------

------------------------------------

**Time and place** ----------------------------------

**Intention** ------------------------------------

**Date** ----------

SPELL

------------------------------------

------------------------------------

------------------------------------

------------------------------------

# Ritual

# Recipe

# Name of the spell

------------------------------

## Time and place

------------------------------

## Intention

------------------------------

### SPELL

------------------------------
------------------------------
------------------------------
------------------------------
------------------------------
------------------------------

### Date

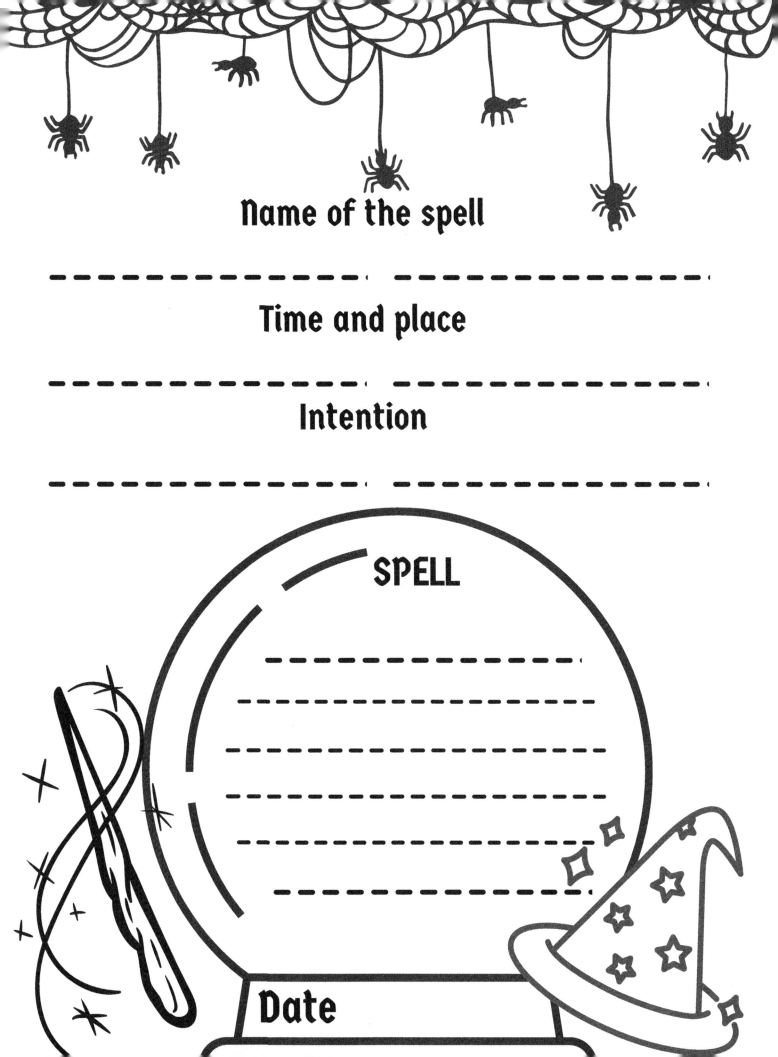

# Ritual

# Recipe

# Name of the spell

------------------------------

------------------------------

**Time and place** ------------------------------

**Intention** ------------------------------

**Date** --------

SPELL

------------------------------

------------------------------

------------------------------

------------------------------

# Ritual

# Recipe

# Name of the spell

- - - - - - - - - - - - - - - - - - - - - - - - - -

## Time and place

- - - - - - - - - - - - - - - - - - - - - - - - - -

## Intention

- - - - - - - - - - - - - - - - - - - - - - - - - -

### SPELL

- - - - - - - - - - - - - - - - - - - -

- - - - - - - - - - - - - - - - - - - -

- - - - - - - - - - - - - - - - - - - -

- - - - - - - - - - - - - - - - - - - -

- - - - - - - - - - - - - - - - - - - -

**Date**

# Ritual

# Recipe

# Name of the spell

------------------------------------

------------------------------------

**Time and place** ------------------------------------

**Intention** ------------------------------------

**Date** ------------

SPELL

------------------------------------

------------------------------------

------------------------------------

------------------------------------

# Ritual

# Recipe

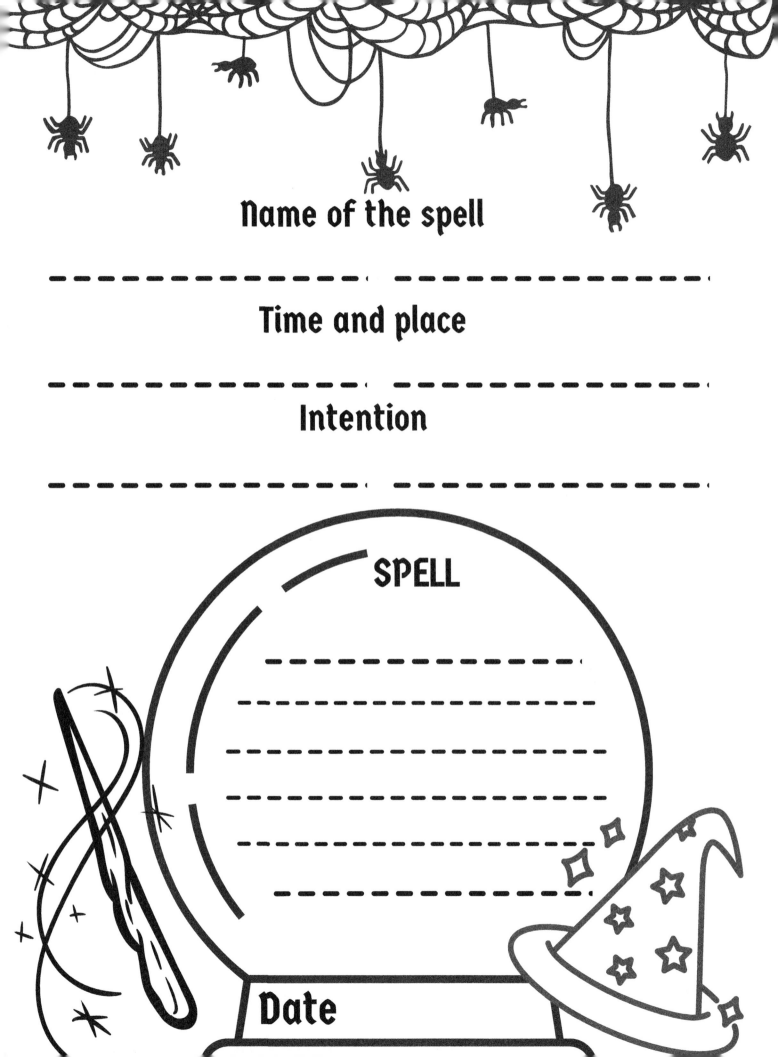

# Name of the spell

-------------------------------------

## Time and place

-------------------------------------

## Intention

-------------------------------------

### SPELL

-------------------------------------
-------------------------------------
-------------------------------------
-------------------------------------
-------------------------------------

### Date

# Ritual

# Recipe

# Name of the spell

------------------------------

------------------------------

**Time and place** ------------------------------

**Intention** ------------------------------

**Date** ----------

SPELL

------------------------------

------------------------------

------------------------------

------------------------------

# Ritual

# Recipe

# Name of the spell

--------------------------------

## Time and place

--------------------------------

## Intention

--------------------------------

### SPELL

--------------------------------

--------------------------------

--------------------------------

--------------------------------

--------------------------------

### Date

# Ritual

# Recipe

# Name of the spell

------------------------------

------------------------------

**Time and place** ------------------------------

**Intention** ------------------------------

**Date** --------

SPELL

------------------------------

------------------------------

------------------------------

------------------------------

# Ritual

# Recipe

# Name of the spell

----------------------------------------

## Time and place

----------------------------------------

## Intention

----------------------------------------

### SPELL

----------------------------------------

----------------------------------------

----------------------------------------

----------------------------------------

----------------------------------------

----------------------------------------

## Date

# Ritual

# Recipe

# Name of the spell

-------------------------------------

-------------------------------------

**Time and place** _____

**Intention** _____

**Date** _____

SPELL

-------------------------------

-------------------------------

-------------------------------

-------------------------------

# Ritual

# Recipe

# Name of the spell

-------------------------------

## Time and place

-------------------------------

## Intention

-------------------------------

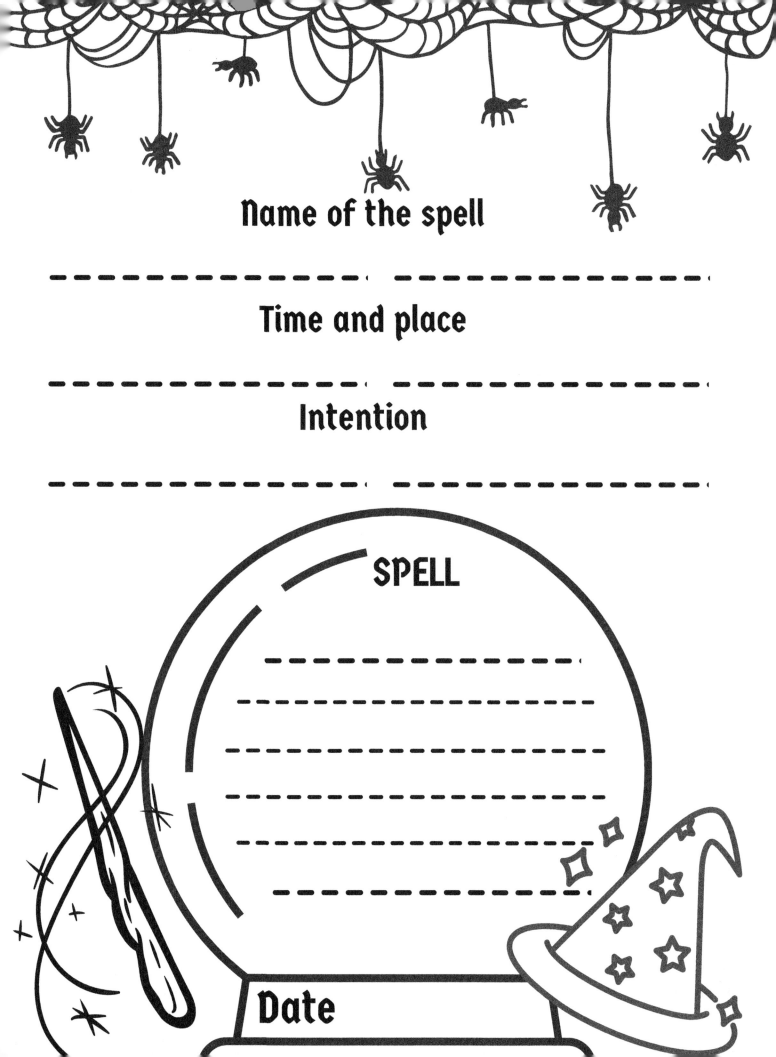

### SPELL

-------------------------------

-------------------------------

-------------------------------

-------------------------------

-------------------------------

-------------------------------

### Date

# Ritual

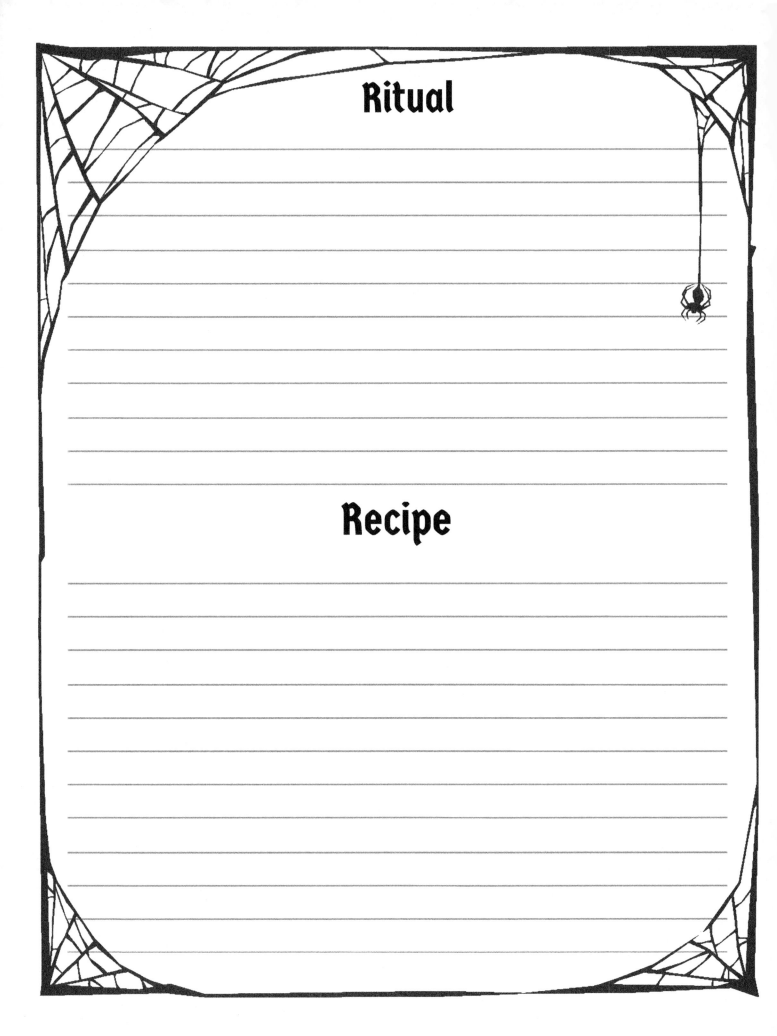

# Recipe

# Name of the spell

------------------------------------

------------------------------------

**Time and place** ------------------------------------

**Intention** ------------------------------------

**Date** ------------

SPELL

------------------------------------

------------------------------------

------------------------------------

------------------------------------

# Ritual

## Recipe

# Name of the spell

----------------------------

## Time and place

----------------------------

## Intention

----------------------------

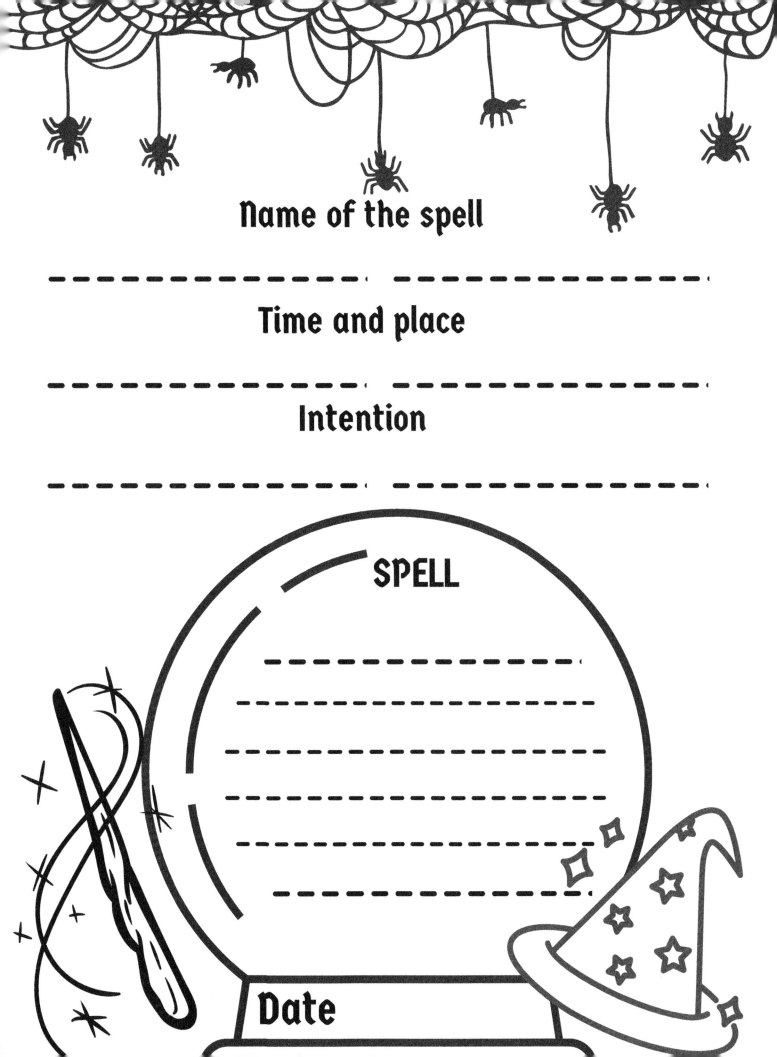

## SPELL

----------------------------

----------------------------

----------------------------

----------------------------

----------------------------

## Date

# Ritual

# Recipe

# Name of the spell

------------------------------

------------------------------

Time and place ------------------------------

Intention ------------------------------

Date ----------

SPELL

------------------------------

------------------------------

------------------------------

------------------------------

# Ritual

# Recipe

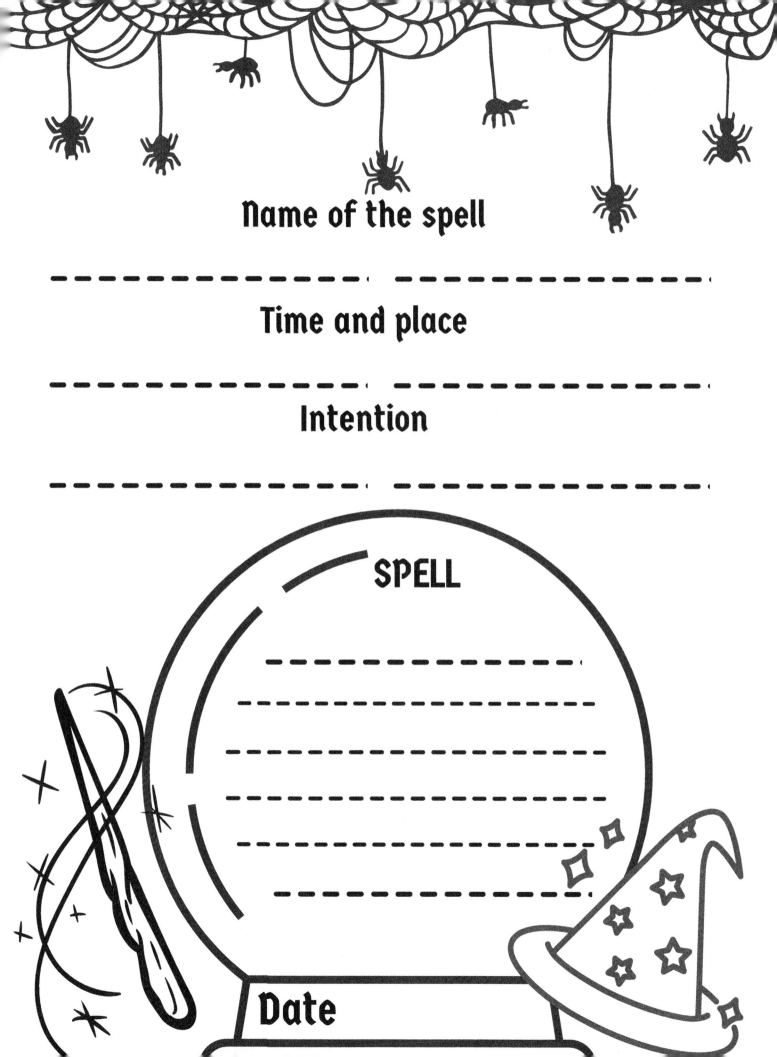

# Name of the spell

- - - - - - - - - - - - - - - - - - - - - - - - - - - - - - -

## Time and place

- - - - - - - - - - - - - - - - - - - - - - - - - - - - - - -

## Intention

- - - - - - - - - - - - - - - - - - - - - - - - - - - - - - -

### SPELL

- - - - - - - - - - - - - - - - - - - - -

- - - - - - - - - - - - - - - - - - - - - -

- - - - - - - - - - - - - - - - - - - - - - -

- - - - - - - - - - - - - - - - - - - - - -

- - - - - - - - - - - - - - - - - - - -

## Date

# Ritual

# Recipe

# Name of the spell

- - - - - - - - - - - - - - - - - - - - - - - - - - - - - -

- - - - - - - - - - - - - - - - - - - - - - - - - - - - - -

**Time and place** - - - - - - - - - - - - - - - - - - - -

**Intention** - - - - - - - - - - - - - - - - -

**Date** - - - - - - -

SPELL

- - - - - - - - - - - - - - - - - - - - - - - -

- - - - - - - - - - - - - - - - - - - - - - - -

- - - - - - - - - - - - - - - - - - - - - - - -

- - - - - - - - - - - - - - - - - - - - - - - -

# Ritual

# Recipe

# Name of the spell

----------------------------------------

## Time and place

----------------------------------------

## Intention

----------------------------------------

### SPELL

----------------------------------------
----------------------------------------
----------------------------------------
----------------------------------------
----------------------------------------
----------------------------------------

### Date

# Ritual

# Recipe

# Name of the spell

----------------------------------------

----------------------------------------

**Time and place** ----------------------------------------

**Intention** ----------------------------------------

**Date** ----------------

SPELL

----------------------------------------

----------------------------------------

----------------------------------------

----------------------------------------

# Ritual

# Recipe

# Name of the spell

------------------------------

## Time and place

------------------------------

## Intention

------------------------------

### SPELL

------------------------------

------------------------------

------------------------------

------------------------------

------------------------------

------------------------------

### Date

# Ritual

# Recipe

# Name of the spell

------------------------------------

------------------------------------

Time and place _____

Intention _____

Date _____

SPELL

------------------------------------

------------------------------------

------------------------------------

------------------------------------

# Ritual

# Recipe

# Name of the spell

- - - - - - - - - - - - - - - - - - - - - - - - - - - - - - -

## Time and place

- - - - - - - - - - - - - - - - - - - - - - - - - - - - - - -

## Intention

- - - - - - - - - - - - - - - - - - - - - - - - - - - - - - -

### SPELL

- - - - - - - - - - - - - - - - - - - -

- - - - - - - - - - - - - - - - - - - - - - -

- - - - - - - - - - - - - - - - - - - - - - - - -

- - - - - - - - - - - - - - - - - - - - - - - - -

- - - - - - - - - - - - - - - - - - - - - - - - -

- - - - - - - - - - - - - - - - - - - -

### Date

# Ritual

# Recipe

# Name of the spell

----------------------------

----------------------------

**Time and place** _____

**Intention** _____

**Date** _____

SPELL

----------------------------

----------------------------

----------------------------

----------------------------

# Ritual

# Recipe

# Name of the spell

----------------------------------------

## Time and place

----------------------------------------

## Intention

----------------------------------------

### SPELL

----------------------------------------

----------------------------------------

----------------------------------------

----------------------------------------

----------------------------------------

----------------------------------------

**Date**

# Ritual

# Recipe

# Name of the spell

----------------------------------

----------------------------------

**Time and place** _____

**Intention** _____

**Date** _____

SPELL

----------------------------------

----------------------------------

----------------------------------

----------------------------------

# Ritual

# Recipe

# Name of the spell

- - - - - - - - - - - - - - - - - - - - - - - - - - - - - - -

## Time and place

- - - - - - - - - - - - - - - - - - - - - - - - - - - - - - -

## Intention

- - - - - - - - - - - - - - - - - - - - - - - - - - - - - - -

### SPELL

- - - - - - - - - - - - - - - - - - - - -

- - - - - - - - - - - - - - - - - - - - -

- - - - - - - - - - - - - - - - - - - - -

- - - - - - - - - - - - - - - - - - - - -

- - - - - - - - - - - - - - - - - - - - -

- - - - - - - - - - - - - - - - - - - - -

## Date

# Ritual

# Recipe

# Name of the spell

-------------------------------

-------------------------------

**Time and place** -------------------------

**Intention** ----------------------------

**Date** --------

SPELL

-------------------------------

-------------------------------

-------------------------------

-------------------------------

# Ritual

# Recipe

# Name of the spell

----------------------

## Time and place

----------------------

## Intention

----------------------

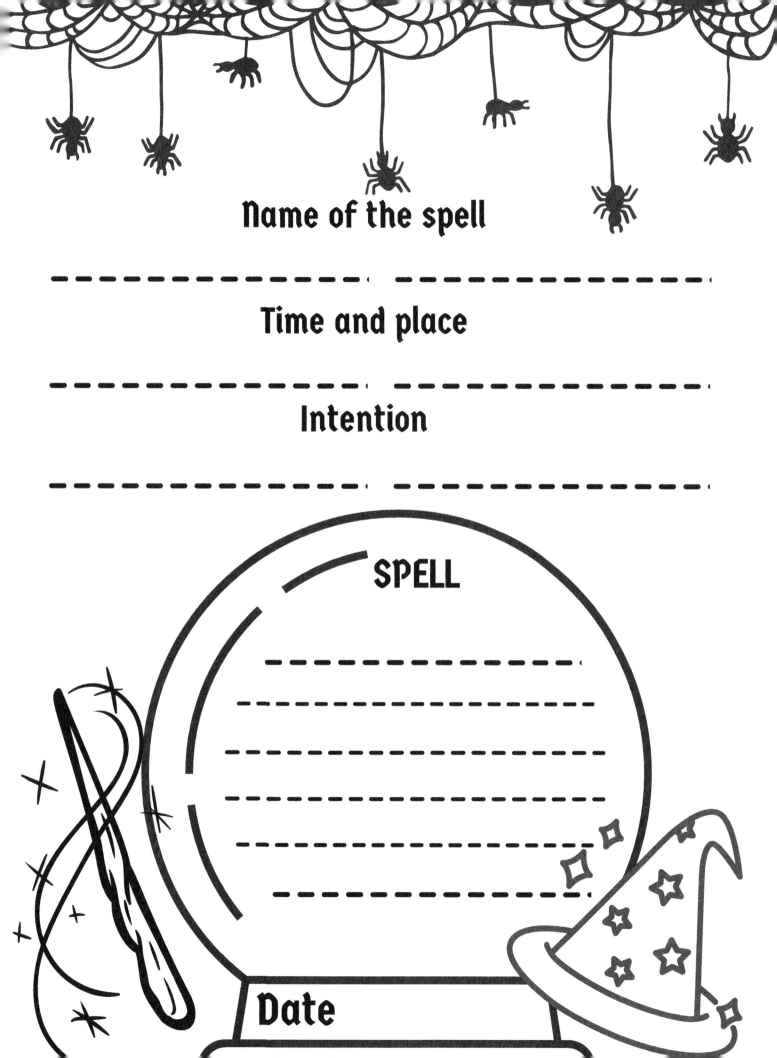

SPELL

------------------------

------------------------

------------------------

------------------------

------------------------

------------------------

Date

# Ritual

# Recipe

# Name of the spell

------------------------------

------------------------------

**Time and place** ----------------------------

**Intention** ----------------------------

**Date** -------

**SPELL**

------------------------------

------------------------------

------------------------------

------------------------------

# Ritual

# Recipe

Name of the spell

-------------------------------------------

Time and place

-------------------------------------------

Intention

-------------------------------------------

SPELL

-------------------------------------------
-------------------------------------------
-------------------------------------------
-------------------------------------------
-------------------------------------------
-------------------------------------------

Date

# Ritual

# Recipe

# Name of the spell

......................................

......................................

**Time and place** ........................................

**Intention** ........................................

**Date** ...........

SPELL

......................................

......................................

......................................

......................................

# Ritual

# Recipe

# Name of the spell

----------------------------------------

## Time and place

----------------------------------------

## Intention

----------------------------------------

## SPELL

----------------------------------------

----------------------------------------

----------------------------------------

----------------------------------------

----------------------------------------

----------------------------------------

## Date

# Ritual

## Recipe

# Name of the spell

------------------------------------

------------------------------------

**Time and place** ----------------------------

**Intention** ----------------------------

**Date** ----------

SPELL

------------------------------------

------------------------------------

------------------------------------

------------------------------------

# Ritual

# Recipe

# Name of the spell

--------------------------------

## Time and place

--------------------------------

## Intention

--------------------------------

### SPELL

--------------------------------
--------------------------------
--------------------------------
--------------------------------
--------------------------------
--------------------------------

## Date

# Ritual

# Recipe

# Name of the spell

------------------------------

------------------------------

**Time and place** ------------------------------

**Intention** ------------------------------

**Date** ----------

**SPELL**

------------------------------

------------------------------

------------------------------

------------------------------

# Ritual

# Recipe

# Name of the spell

- - - - - - - - - - - - - - - - - - - - - - - - - - - - - - - - - -

## Time and place

- - - - - - - - - - - - - - - - - - - - - - - - - - - - - - - - - -

## Intention

- - - - - - - - - - - - - - - - - - - - - - - - - - - - - - - - - -

## SPELL

- - - - - - - - - - - - - - - - -

- - - - - - - - - - - - - - - - - - - - -

- - - - - - - - - - - - - - - - - - - - -

- - - - - - - - - - - - - - - - - - - - -

- - - - - - - - - - - - - - - - -

## Date

# Ritual

# Recipe

# Name of the spell

-------------------------------------

-------------------------------------

**Time and place** -------------------------------------

**Intention** -------------------------------------

**Date** -----------

SPELL

-------------------------------------

-------------------------------------

-------------------------------------

-------------------------------------

# Ritual

# Recipe

# Name of the spell

------------------------------------------------

## Time and place

------------------------------------------------

## Intention

------------------------------------------------

### SPELL

------------------------------------

------------------------------------

------------------------------------

------------------------------------

------------------------------------

**Date**

# Ritual

# Recipe

# Notes

# Notes

# Notes

# Notes

# Notes

# Notes

# Notes

# Notes

# Notes

# Notes

# Notes

# Notes

# Notes

# Notes

Printed in Great Britain
by Amazon

69231092R10059